RHYTHMIC COMPOSITION

Featuring the music of Porcupine Tree
By Gavin Harrison and Terry Branam

Transcriptions by Terry Branam
Music engraving and page layout by Terry Branam
Cover design by Terry Branam
Cover photo by Lasse Hoile
Additional text editing by Joe Bergamini

DISTRIBUTED BY

HAL•LEONARD®
CORPORATION

7777 W. BLUEMOUND RD. P.O. BOX 13819
MILWAUKEE, WISCONSIN 53213

HUDSON
LIMITED™
A DIVISION OF HUDSON MUSIC, LLC.

Contents

Contents

Mastery and Mystery
By Neil Peart

Calling Gavin Harrison "a great drummer" seems insufficient, even a case of "damning with faint praise." These days plenty of guys, and some girls, can demonstrate amazing technical prowess and speed on a drumset. Instead, I would call Gavin a great *musician*. His formidable technique and deeply analytical approach to drumset-playing are always focused on a simple purpose: serving the song.

His discography is dizzying in its variety, clearly representing a player who is able to be sympathetic in a great many disparate styles. He would never disrupt a vocalist's phrasing, or disturb a soloist's spotlight, yet he will always *energize* them — feed in currents of rhythmic electricity that elevate the *whole*, not just the drum part.

My introduction to Gavin's drumming was on a sampler CD made for me in the early 2000s by my dear friend Matt Scannell, from Vertical Horizon. From time to time Matt used to make me a playlist of music he had encountered that he thought was . . . worth my attention. "You may not *love* it," he would stress, but he thought it seemed important to know about. I understood, and listened accordingly.

One of those CDs included a couple of tracks from Porcupine Tree's early masterpiece, *In Absentia* (2002), namely "Trains" and "The Sound of Muzak."

Well. Of course I know there is no way two songs can begin to hint at the breadth of Gavin's virtuosity, but I have to say — those two drum tracks offer a hell of a start!

The timekeeping in "Trains" gracefully smoothes over what could be a jagged combination of rhythms, while also planting strategic crash cymbals to help "orient" the listener. The fills toward the end are ingenious, not only musically, or even technically, but as pure listening *excitement* — taking the listener out to the edge of comprehension, seemingly the edge of control, across the time and straight through the middle of it. Yet they deliver us right back to the perfect "one" — feeling as though we have been on a carnival ride.

In contrast, the groove-making on "The Sound of Muzak" applies a more laid-back attitude — still intricate, meticulous, and intensely musical, but with a more relaxed feel. The listener is led "comfortably" through a complex rhythmic landscape with well-defined directional signals and milestones. The transitional fills are richly percussive and melodic — a combination of tuning and touch that is the hallmark of a deeply sensitive player.

Foreword

Later, after hearing more of Porcupine Tree's music, and enjoying it — *appreciating* it — very much, I watched some of Gavin's instructional material. Hearing him expound on the way he worked, I was fairly astonished to learn that he had arrived at some of these "conclusions" by means that seemed entirely alien to me. Hearing the assemblage of his fiery fills and intricate accompaniments, I would think, "Yes — if I could play like that, that is how I would play."

But when I heard Gavin explain the thinking, the tools, the "machinery" that had led him to these expressions, I was kind of shocked. Onscreen, he would demonstrate some ridiculously complicated pattern, then say something like, "Now I will displace that rhythm by a sixteenth note."

"Ha ha," I would think, funny joke, right? But did he not proceed to play exactly that? (Near as I could tell, anyway — I never was good at maths.)

That observation alone was profound to me. The music Gavin created seemed entirely "relatable," even "organic" — constructed from a seemingly natural feel for rhythmic subdivisions, dynamics, controlled time feels (sometimes relaxed, other times aggressive), tension and release, techniques like triplet-feel fills slashing across straight-time passages — the "tools of the trade" for a master drummer. However, behind all that, the means Gavin had used to develop those ideas were completely foreign, completely opaque to me.

And isn't that wonderful?

Nothing wrong with "painting by numbers," that's for sure ("whatever gets you back to 'one'"), but I have always worked more by trial-and-error, thinking of phrases in a more "conversational" way. Yet I believe I at least *aim for* the same style of expression and energetic punctuation that Gavin delivers with such seemingly effortless poise. As mountaineers would express it, there are "many routes to the summit."

But what's most important in the context of Gavin's drumming is that you don't need to be aware of *any* of that to have your pulse raised — to be *inspired* by his excellent example. You don't need to know the recipe to enjoy the meal, or know the formula to feel good from the medicine.

A poet in ancient Rome said, "If the art is concealed, it succeeds."

That principle not only reflects the previous analysis, but leads to another

Foreword

illumination — how subtly integrated Gavin's drum parts are with the orchestration.

Of course, Porcupine Tree is not the only "stage" on which Gavin has excelled. His studio work, as mentioned, is wide ranging and vast. The touring work, too — Level 42, for example, certainly a demanding rhythm section to join, following the sublime "pocket" and highly musical flourishes of Phil Gould (not to mention the phenomenal Gary Husband), interlocking with the powerful virtuosity of Mark King.

And more recently, to have been found worthy to play in an elite organization like King Crimson. What a heritage of drummers in that band! From the brilliant and ground-breaking Michael Giles, one of my own earliest and biggest influences, through Ian Wallace, Bill Bruford, and Pat Mastellotto, and now Gavin will be working on new material with the latest lineup of that legendarily inventive ensemble.

So there will be more drumming excitement to look forward to from Gavin Harrison, and I for one will be listening with interest, and a little bemusement.

Maybe I should have paid more attention in math class?

About This Book

This book documents my work with Porcupine Tree so far. I've tried to recall as many relevant things as possible about these recordings and the way in which they were made. Including the live touring, this spans eight pretty intense years of my life. Porcupine Tree is a progressive band, and it's easy for me to see the evolution of what we've achieved over this time. Where I can, I've made specific notes about the concepts behind the rhythms I played, the drums I used, and the studios we recorded in.

For those of you who may have seen any of my previous books and DVDs, you'll know that I like to design rhythmic parts from the ground up. Nothing excites me more than finding a unique signature drum part for a song. In fact, the drum part becomes part of the composition. I feel that my job as a drummer is similar to that of an architect or structural engineer; there are many parallels in the way that I construct rhythms for songs. If you were designing a building, for instance, you could just draw a square box, put in some windows, a door, a roof, and call it a building. This would satisfy all the basic requirements of a building, but there's no beauty to it. Great design is to see beauty beyond the

functional. A drum part, like a building, can still be functional while having elegance, style and sophistication. But, if you get too fancy, you could tip the balance to the point of it not working as a functional building anymore.

Design is about balance, and it can be a delicate thing. However, it's your sense of taste that will decide when the balance is right. Of course, your sense of taste and character can change over time. The famous lyrics of Tower of Power state: "What is hip today might become passé," so you need to constantly re-examine your definition of "hip." For instance, you might put on a gold chain around your neck and think it looks great. If you put on ten gold chains, does it look ten times better?

Drumming has changed a lot over the last hundred years thanks to many great innovators. Rather than simply supplying a dull background thud that indicates the tempo, the contemporary drummer has many more interesting ways in which he/she can interact with the other instruments. Drummers can also contribute to the structure of the composition, affecting the overall sound of the band, but one must not forget the focus of the song: the melody. The song (or a certain section of it) might only require a dull background thud. If that's the best part to play, then you just need to recognize it, free of ego. Sometimes the best part is to not play at all. If it enhances the song, then it's a really good drum part.

About The Transcriptions

Transcribing has always been a labor of love for me; it's as if I get to take a lesson with my favorite drummers and get inside their thought process at the same time. *Rhythmic Composition* has been an incredible learning experience and an enormous challenge. Having studied Gavin's previous books and DVDs, I was able to understand many of the concepts that went into his drum parts. However, finding the true intention behind the notes is always the bigger goal for me. Through working on this project with Gavin, my own musical approach has been greatly influenced through the intense listening that was required. As you will see, these rhythms and time signatures can be interpreted in a variety of ways. I've had to settle on the ones that are easiest to comprehend, while keeping a close eye/ear on Gavin's "intentions."

As for the technical end of things, I use Finale software to do my transcriptions. I also choose to transcribe in real time, as opposed to using software to slow things down. I feel that developing your ear to hear things in "real time" is the best way to really grasp what is happening in that very moment, as it was intended to be played. I hope that these transcriptions are beneficial to you not only to study the music of Porcupine Tree, but also to assist in unlocking your own creative spirit. Good luck!

Terry Branam
May, 2013

Equipment

My equipment is constantly evolving, so I can only accurately list a drumset at a given point in time. I could list exactly what I'm playing right now, but by the time you read this, things may have changed a bit.

I have been proudly playing Sonor drums (since 2001), Zildjian cymbals (since 1986), Vic Firth sticks (since the late 1980s), and Remo heads (since 1979). The basic shape of my drumset hasn't changed that much for about 25 years. That is to say: 3 small rack toms (8", 10" 12") and two floor toms (14", 16" and more recently 15", 18"), a 22" bass drum, a 14"x5" snare drum, and a 12"x5" snare drum. At the moment, I'm using a Gibraltar rack, Porter & Davies tactile monitor stool, Hardcase drum cases, as well as Tama Speed Cobra pedals and Cobra clutch.

Notation Key

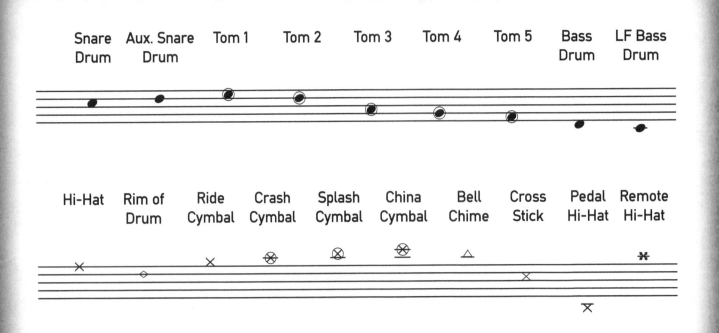

Articulation Key

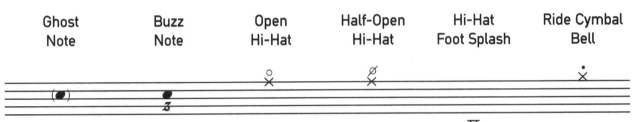

Chapter 1

In Absentia

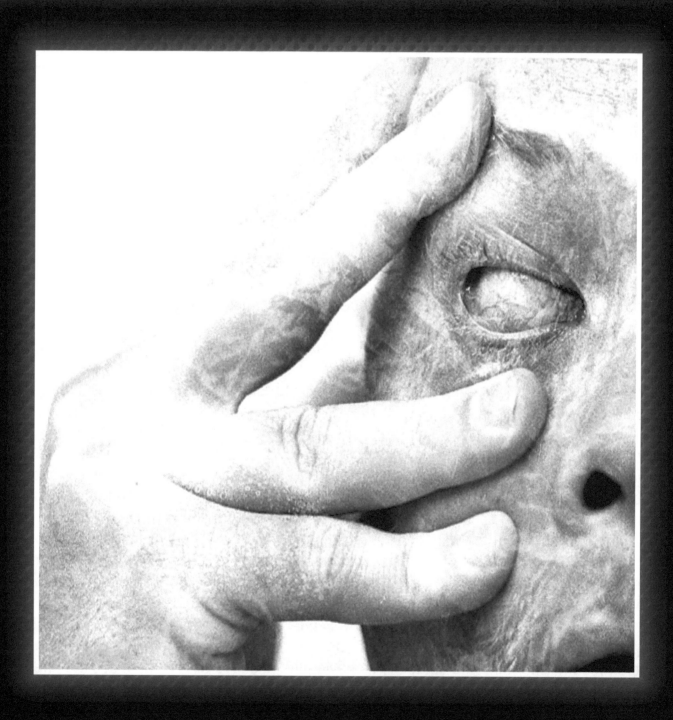

In Absentia

The *In Absentia* record was made at Avatar (Power Station) studios in Manhattan, New York. It was a strange time to be there because it was so soon after the 9/11 disaster. In fact, I believe we were there on the six month anniversary. I got to stay in a very nice hotel close to Times Square. It was a really nice buzz to walk through the streets of Manhattan every morning "on my way to work," and go to one of the best studios in the world. It has an absolutely legendary large wood drum room that lets the drums really sing out. The drums sound quite different compared to other PT recordings partly because of the acoustics in that particular room. Tim Palmer (who mixed it) also used a lot of compression and eq to really bring out the room mics.

Everyone felt very excited about being at Avatar. The drums sounded amazing in that place, and engineer Paul Northfield did a great job. We originally wanted to record the drums directly to two-inch 24-track analog tape, and we bought in about twenty reels of the stuff (at enormous cost). We devised an experiment for the first song: we simultaneously recorded to tape and to the computer hard drive through digital converters. We then listened carefully to the results—and the digital path unanimously won! I was quite relieved about that, because as a drummer, there's more pressure recording to tape, as the possibilities of dropping in and out of "record" are very limiting. All the sessions that I had done from 1980 to the late 1990s had been onto tape, so I knew that I'd have to nail the whole song in one pass. If there were moments in my performance that I didn't love, I'd just have to live with it. The same is not true of the other instruments (when recording onto analog tape). They are usually recorded with just one or two mics (or DI boxes), and certainly not with the massive ambience of a live room and the twenty mics that the drumset would have on it.

My method of recording to hard drive hasn't changed much in the last twenty years. First, I will rehearse the song for as long as I want. Next, I might do some test recordings for the sound so I can be sure the drums and cymbals are the right ones for the piece, and try out some ideas for certain sections. Once I feel happy that I've got all the parts and the sounds right, I begin recording "for real." I can tell as I'm playing if it's a "keeper take" or not, so I quite often do a few false starts and instantly erase them as I go. There's very little point continuing if you don't get off to a great start. I'm looking to have about four complete takes that I'm happy with. Usually with the last pass (knowing that I've pretty much already got it "in the bag"), I might try some different and wild things just in case some happy accidents happen that I might be able to edit in later. Then I listen through all the takes and make notes. Usually, one will stand out to me as having the best overall feel, so that's the one I'll use. I might edit in some things from any of the other takes if they were better than on the

In Absentia

"good feeling" take. This is where recording at home has some nice advantages: you have no time pressure and it's not costing anything. Some days I feel more or less inspired than others, so if I think it might be better to go out and ride my bike and come back to it tomorrow, I easily can.

Editing the takes immediately after I've done them is also a really good idea. Occasionally I will edit the drum takes and still feel like something is missing at some point in the song. Then it's easy to go over to the drums and work on that part; nothing has changed. The sound of the drums and the tuning haven't moved and the mics are still all in exactly the same place.

Recording at home is an interesting thing. It's very comfortable and familiar, of course, but it lacks the interaction with other band members or engineers. I'm completely on my own all day. There's isn't a feeling of "going to work," which I occasionally miss. On the other hand, it's pressure-free, and possibly some of my best results have come from working at home. It's hard to say which method I prefer.

There's also something very nice about recording in interesting locations—they can put you in a certain mood. I remember making a record in Paris and feeling uplifted walking through the streets on my way to the studio. Something about the atmosphere just makes you feel different—it's exciting.

Feeling that way can make you play differently. I've had similar sensations recording in Berlin in 1986 (when the city was still surrounded by the wall), Rome, Milan, LA, and even in my home town of London.

Above all, I've learned this lesson many times when approaching performance: Being mentally ready makes a lot more difference than being physically ready.

Blackest Eyes

This was the first song we recorded on the second day of the *In Absentia* sessions. We spent the first day just setting up, sound checking, and conducting our "analog tape experiment." I would generally get to the studio in the morning before the other guys, and start warming up for 20-30 minutes. When it came to recording, Colin played bass (in the control room) along with me, but I don't think any of it was kept. I believe he re-did all of the bass tracks after I went home. For my part, I had worked with the demos at home for a week or so before I came to NYC. I would start by listening to my minidisc player (remember those things?) to hear some ideas that I had recorded. I was using two hi-hats for the *In Absentia* recording as well as the following tour. The auxillary hi-hat was set up to the right of my leg, where a floor tom would normally be, but a bit closer to me.

The verses of this song are played on two hi-hats. I'm mostly riding on the right (tightly closed) hi-hat, while the left hand hits the snare drum, and occasionally the left hi-hat. The snare hits on beat "3e" of the verse bars were mostly played on a slightly smaller snare drum that was off to the left of my main hi-hat. It's quite a subtle sound difference between the two snares, so when we played it live, I didn't bother with it. I decided to use two hi-hats in my set up because of a song called "The Creator has a Mastertape." When I rehearsed it at home I couldn't think of a better way to play that song other than with the extra hi-hat. I don't think I used an auxillary hi-hat other than on those two songs, so after we stopped playing "The Creator" live, I switched back to my normal single-hi-hat setup.

Blackest Eyes

♩=95

Steven Wilson

Intro

Verse

Chorus

Blackest Eyes

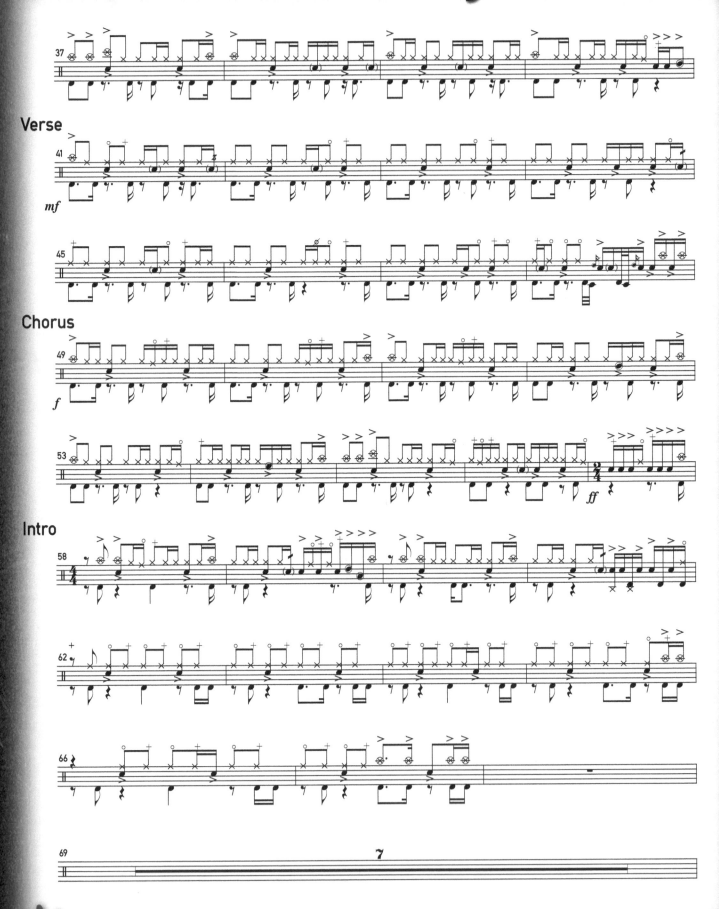

Verse

Chorus

Intro

Blackest Eyes

Chorus

Outro

Trains

There's something quirky about the way that the chords move in this song. Initially it confused me. The root chord lands on the "2&" of the 4/4 bar. When I first heard the demo of this song, I assumed that this was the downbeat, and wrote out a drum chart with alternating bars of 3/8 and 5/8—which looked pretty strange on paper. Having written books about *Rhythmic Illusions* and how you can twist and manipulate the perception of the listener, I fell straight into my own rhythmically twisted hole from the very first time I heard the song! Maybe that's what Steve intended, but I didn't ask him at the time. When we started to rehearse it for our first live shows later in 2002, something about it didn't sound quite right. We abandoned the song and didn't get around to playing it live until a few years later—by which time I had figured it out in straight 4/4. It's hard when you hear something one way and then try to re-learn it another way.

PT songs are full of little rhythmic and melodic illusions. It's something that has caught us all out at some point—usually resulting in a very amazed/confused face at a rehearsal when someone explains where the "real downbeat" is.

When we finally did start playing "Trains" live, it was very popular with our fans. I think it might be our most-played song to date. It became a lot of fun to play as a final encore. For some reason, I started doing a magic trick towards the end of the song (when the drums drop out in the live version). At first I would hold up a towel and pretend that something was pushing it's way mystically through the middle. It was (of course) a drumstick held and manipulated in my right hand. It wasn't meant to be a really convincing magic trick, but, unbelievably, people would actually ask me (in genuine amazement) how I did it!

Trains

Here's the original chart that I made for "Trains":

Trains

♩=87

Steven Wilson

@ 1:06

Verse

Chorus

Guitar Solo

Chorus

Trains

+ Vocals

@ 4:46

The Sound of Muzak

This is one of the songs that I get asked about a lot, and one that I get a lot of requests to play at drum clinics. I can't take too much credit for it (even if it does get assigned to me), because it's a drum rhythm that Steve wrote on a drum machine. It's an interesting groove because of the way that it fits with the guitar riff, as well as the fact that it's made up of all sevens. When I'm presented with a demo that has a drum machine on it, I will usually listen to it once and then turn it off so I can think of something to play. Occasionally, I'll hear something that a "non-drummer" has programmed and think, "That's a great part." I'm not too proud to recognize a really good rhythm that fits a tune perfectly. I'm more than happy to go along with it, even if I didn't invent it. Some folks might even think it was my idea!

The bass drum to snare drum pattern is in fact 7/16, but I always thought of it as 7/8. There is a quarter-note override accented on the hi-hat that gives it a 7/4 feel. So there you have it: 7/16, 7/8, and 7/4. I've seen people arguing about the correct time signature of this song, but it really doesn't matter—it's seven which ever way you think about it. I can, however, take credit for the subtleties and nuances of the groove. I think that it has evolved slightly over the years that I've been playing it. For example, I play more ghost notes inside the pattern now than I did originally. I always want to try and make it sound as smooth as possible. Sometimes odd time signatures can come across a bit awkward and jerky. In this case, the quarter-note override on the hi-hat really helps to smooth things out. I've seen people dancing along to it at concerts. I imagine that they don't really know what the time signature is, and this is my point: it doesn't actually matter as long as you can enjoy the song. Most people don't care where the bar lines are, as long as they can relate to the music in some way.

Andy Karp in full air-drumming mode.

I remember an interviewer saying to me that he couldn't believe how laid-back I played the chorus in this song. It never really struck me before, because I always try to play that way. I'm always trying to make things sound relaxed and comfortable, even when it's an odd time signature.

Thinking back to the recording sessions, I can remember that it was the first song that we played on the third day. My mind was in just the right place. I had really settled in and was feeling good. The band, Paul Northfield (engineer), Andy Leff (manager), and Andy Karp (record company), were all watching through the control room window. I only did a couple of takes. The first one went really well, and I believe that's the one that we used. It had a fresh, inspired feeling about it.

The Sound of Muzak

♩=95

Steven Wilson

Verse

mf

Pre-Chorus

Chorus

f

Verse

mf

The Sound of Muzak

Pre-Chorus

Chorus

Solo Section

The Sound of Muzak

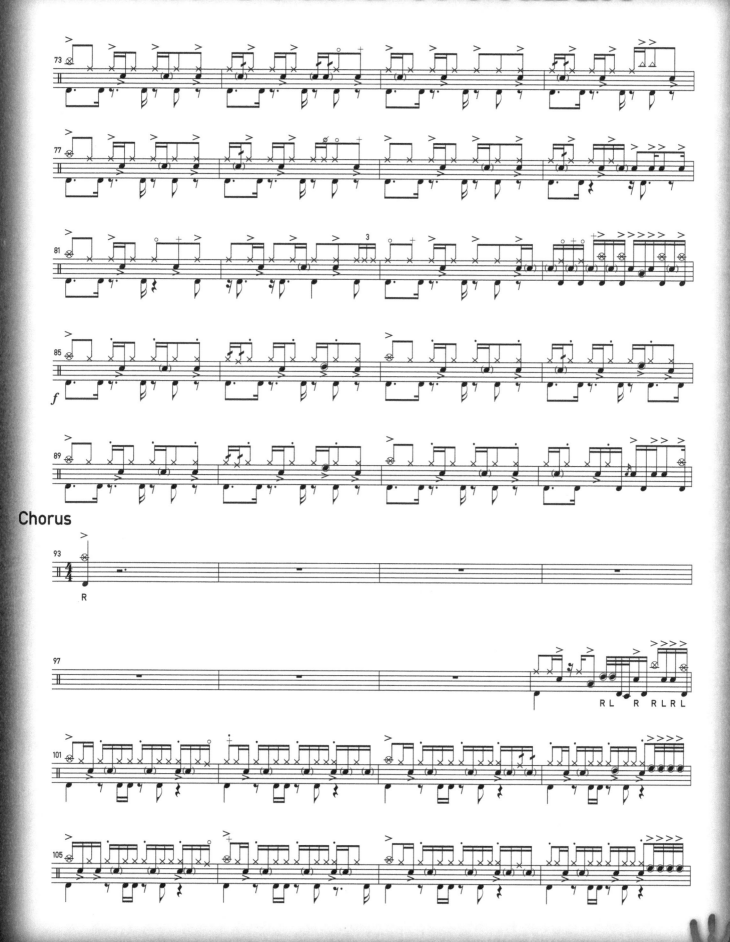

Chorus

The Sound of Muzak

There's always plenty of waiting to do on tour.

Chapter 2

Futile

Porcupine tree
FUTILE

Futile

This song started as an idea I had while on a plane journey home from Greece in 2002. It was early on in my time in the band—in fact not long after the recording of *In Absentia*. I had a series of drum clinics coming up in Italy, and I was thinking of playing a really heavy song that was very rhythmically involved. Before I joined PT, I hadn't played much "metal" music. Steve had introduced me to the music of the Swedish band Meshuggah, and I was really impressed. Having always been a fan of a good "rhythmic design," these guys were taking it to some beautiful places. I couldn't stop listening to *Destroy Erase Improve*. It was by far the heaviest thing I'd ever heard at that point. I used to play it for friends of mine

(jazz and prog musicians) who I knew had never been exposed to such types of music, and they were blown away. On that flight home I asked Steve, "Can you come over to my house with your guitar? I've got an idea for a drum clinic song and I need some help with it." I had already written the intro section (bars 16-27) with the arpeggiating notes, and I wanted it to sound like it was in 12/8 (even though it was a rhythmic illusion and actually all in 4/4). I had also improvised some syncopated, jerky math-metal phrases to go along with it. Steve and I went through those and edited together the best ones. He then could add some low metal guitar notes to fit with them (bars 11-15). Whenever I played this song, I would play the whole thing to a quarter-note click.

There is a verse section that has quarter notes on the hi-hat and syncopated sixteenth-note anticipations on the bass drum and snare drum. It sounds like they are displaced from the main hi-hat pulse (bars 28-51). Basically, the whole song is in 4/4, apart from one recurring bar in the chorus which is in 3/4, as well as one 5/4 bar near the end.

I had never imagined this being a PT song, but Steve said he would take it home and work on it. A few days later, he sent me a new version that he'd written lyrics to. He also added a great bridge section (bar 112) where the guitar is playing patterns of ascending 5/16. The whole song had really taken on a new vibe. I felt like the best idea for me was to just hold down a 4/4 pattern throughout all of that rather than pick out the patterns of five that the guitar was playing. Once Colin and Richard added their parts, the song really came to life, and we thought it would be fun to play live. The first time that we played it was in Tampa, Florida in July of 2003, and we continued playing it all through the following tour that we did with Opeth. There's a very good desk recording of it from our show at the Astoria in London later that year. I think that's pretty much the last time we played it. It was the kind of tune that we needed to play and rehearse every day in order for it to sound good. It was probably the hardest piece that we had ever tried to play at that point.

Futile

Unlike the tracks from *In Absentia* which were recorded at Avatar in NYC, I recorded the drums for this song at home. That triggered the idea of recording the next two PT albums (*Deadwing* and *Fear Of A Blank Planet*) the same way. I remember using my late 1940s Avedis Zildjian 20" ride (which was really a big band ride cymbal) that I got from my late drum teacher Joe Hodson. It's a bit ironic to play death metal on it, but it had such a great bell I couldn't resist using it. I played that ride cymbal on a lot of PT recordings right up until I broke it while recording "Time Flies" from *The Incident*. I also played my Noble & Cooley 14"x5" alloy snare drum on that recording. The drums were my Sonor Designer earth finish kit.

I made a version of this song to play on the 2008 Modern Drummer Festival where I looped the 4/4 guitar riff from the intro so that I could play a drum solo over it; I have never played that version since. My good friend Laurence Cottle made an amazing big band version of this song that I've played many times at drum clinics. There's also a good version of it on YouTube from a clinic in Chesham, UK in 2011.

Futile

♩=112

Steven Wilson, Gavin Harrison

Futile

Chorus

Verse

Futile

Chorus

Riff

Futile

Bridge

Riff

Chorus

Futile

Riff

Outro

Chapter 3

Deadwing

Deadwing

We waited longer than we really wanted to make this record because there were a lot of changes happening within the record company. Many folks were leaving and our label guys were either getting fired or re-shuffled.

We knew that we were going to have to find a different way to record *Deadwing*. Thanks to the experiment of "Futile" and the very rare "Orchidia," the other guys were happy to have me record the drums in my home studio. In fact, the band writing session also happened there. We were also persuaded to make an updated version of "She'sMovedOn" which is on the American release of the album—although not listed because it was meant to be a secret track. This came about because an important DJ said that the song was his favorite, and if we re-recorded it and put it on the album, he would play it to death on his radio station. To my recollection that never happened.

I have often been asked about a couple of fills on that tune. The first one happens at 0:30:

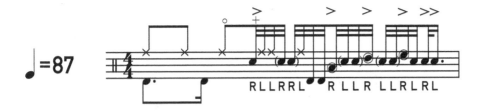

The other one is at 3:18:

Apart from all the songs on *Deadwing*, there were some other interesting tracks that came out as B-sides: "Mother and Child Divided" and "So Called Friend".

The drumset would have been my Sonor Designer earth finish kit: 22x16 bass drum; 8x8, 10x8, 12x9, 14x12, and 16x14 toms. The snare drums would have been my old Yamaha 1982 Recording Custom 14x5, a Noble & Cooley Alloy 14x5, and a Sonor Designer 12x5. The cymbals were Zildjians: 13" K hi-hats, 18" K Custom crashes, 8" EFX, 12" Oriental Trash china, a late 1940's 20" ride, 15" K Custom crash, and an 18" Z china.

The microphones were a Beyer M88 in the bass drum, EV408s on the toms, Shure SM57 on top and bottom of the snare drum, AKG CK391s on the hi-hat and ride, a pair of Royer 122s as overheads, and a pair of Scheops CMC5s for big room ambience.

Halo

"Halo" started life as a drum experiment which turned into the middle section of the tune (the 17/16 part). Basically, I had come up with some tom and snare drum melodies during an improvisation session that equaled 5/16 + 5/16 + 7/16. I exchanged the tom hits for bass drum hits, and then played a quarter-note override on the hi-hat. This idea came from a drum DVD that I had made the year before, *Rhythmic Horizons*. I showed the band the rhythm, and the way the bass line followed the 5+5+7 pattern. They liked it. We worked on it for an hour or so before we said, "Ok, what shall we do with it?" Richard had a keyboard sequencer set up playing a syncopated sixteenth-note 4/4 pattern. I just started jamming along with it. Colin worked out a catchy bass line and we were starting to have a good vibe. Steve took the whole thing away with him and stitched it all together into the song that you now know.

The song became a regular fixture in the set, and is what we would close the show with. We've apparently played the song live 240 times. I remember playing it in LA at the Wilshire Theatre and seeing my buddy Danny Carey (the drummer of Tool) sitting in the third row. I thought, "Wow, he's going to dig this middle section in 17/16." I completely screwed it up! There's a lesson in there about getting distracted!

When we decided to play it live, I suggested that we could extend the intro section. To start, the sequencer plays for eight bars, then I would join in and play the groove over the next eight measures. During the tour, the fills that I played to bring the band in on bar 17 were getting more and more outrageous every night. It was one of those moments when we knew we could have a laugh and do something different. I was just trying to save myself from going completely nuts.

When I joined Porcupine Tree, the guys were quite surprised after the first few nights that I didn't play the exact same thing in the same place every performance. I remember them saying, "You played completely different tonight." I took that as a compliment because that is what I was trying to do. There are basically two different camps of thought over playing live: Camp A believes that the fills and solos on the record have become part of the composition, therefore the parts should faithfully be reproduced as close to the original as possible, because they think that's what the audience expects and wants to hear. So, let's play the concert exactly as the record every night. Camp B, however, feels that every solo and drum fill should be improvised night after night. It would mean that each concert would be a unique experience. The audience would appreciate something different from the record along with the effort and creativity that it shows to invent new stuff all the time. It stops you from going mad in an endless repetitive "Groundhog Day" cycle. I appear to be mostly in Camp B–although there are some fills that I think are important to the arrangement. I think the band and audience are expecting to hear them, so I keep those in. I think there is no right or wrong between Camp A or B, or anywhere in between. They are all perfectly valid.

Halo

Here's an excerpt from the *Rhythmic Horizons* DVD eBook showing how a pattern that started life as an exercise in odd groupings and (quarter-note and then dotted-eighth-note) overrides on the hi-hat eventually evolved into the bridge section of "Halo" (Override Ex. 20 and 21):

Override Ex. 20

Override Ex. 21

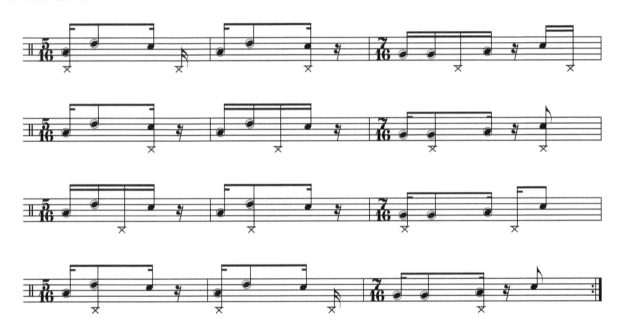

Override Ex. 22

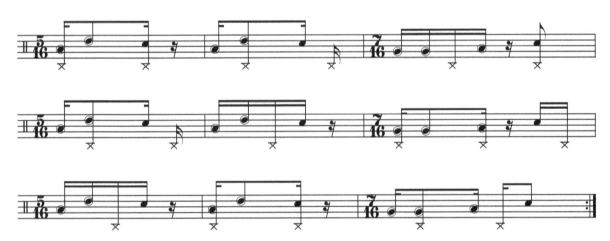

Halo

♩=98

Steven Wilson, Gavin Harrison,
Richard Barbieri, Colin Edwin

Verse

Pre-Chorus

Chorus

Halo

Verse

Pre-Chorus

Chorus

Bridge

Halo

Lazarus

"Lazarus" is a nice, simple song that Steve brought to the band. I took a very straightforward approach to it, like a classic pop song. It didn't feel that it needed anything else. Sometimes the best drum part is to play something that stays out of the way and keeps the focus on the vocals. I did get to come up with a slightly unusual fill (bar 56). I liked the way that the three thirty-second notes came from the ground up (bass drum to floor tom to snare drum).

This song was welcomed and favored by the small percentage of females in the audience. There's something about progressive rock or perhaps odd time signatures that most ladies don't really dig. I would say that it's a very risky strategy to bring a potential girlfriend to a prog rock show. It could be the "End of Something Beautiful!"

Lazarus

♩=86

Steven Wilson

Chorus @ 0:45

Verse

Chorus

Bridge

Lazarus

Chorus

Open Car

This song starts with an interesting rhythm from the guitar and vocals that also forms part of the verse. Basically it's groups of 5/16 + 5/16 + 7/16 (which is actually the same as the middle section of "Halo"). Hearing this for the first time, I scratched my chin and looked out the window, wondering what to play to such a collection of notes. This scene might have looked better if I'd been smoking a pipe and looking out to sea (Ok, we'll save that for the film). Should I follow it and play all of those fives and sevens, or maybe pick out just some of them? Maybe I could play another rhythm in seventeen that would counter-balance what Steve was doing?

Of course the fun of having a studio at home is that I can try all of those things (and many more) to see what they sound like. In the end, I opted for a 4/4-sounding rhythm that would make Steve's part sound more syncopated. I just needed to disguise the end of the second bar of my 4/4 beat to incorporate another eighth note without disturbing the 4/4 feel.

When we recorded this song, there was another sixteen-bar section after the second verse (at bar 35). For some reason that I can't remember, we dropped it for the album cut. It was an instrumental section that had a bit of double-bass drumming and a keyboard solo in it. When we came to play this song after the album was released, we reinstated the section. You can hear it on the live recording *Arriving Somewhere.*

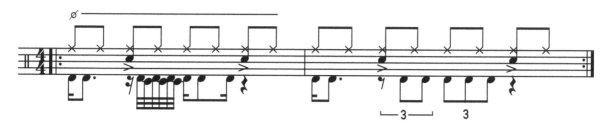

It's also true that when you hear the songs on our concert recordings, you can hear how much the drum parts and fills have evolved since the original recording.

Open Car

♩=80

Steven Wilson

Verse

Pre-Chorus

Chorus

Verse

Open Car

Pre-Chorus

Chorus

Start of Something Beautiful

This is another song that started with some drum ideas. I had previously bought an album of an artist who normally does a few nice odd-meter tunes. One song on this person's album was in 9/4, with a drum machine groove, but I really didn't like the beat that was programmed. I played along to see if I could find a part that I liked better. I eventually stumbled across the basic outline of the beat that I use on "Start of Something Beautiful."

One day Steve was at my place, and I played him some of my ideas. I'd been working on a groove in 9/4 that had spacious backbeats, with a slow, laid-back feeling that worked in contrast with a much more hectic pattern in 5/4. Originally I called the song "9 to 5," but I guess Dolly Parton's lawyers might have had a problem with that! Steve picked up my bass guitar and started to jam along. We discussed the contrast of the two grooves. Maybe the nine part could be a verse, and the five part could be a chorus? The song was born. We found this song very challenging to play live. It takes a lot of concentration to make it sound good.

I can hear a good bit of Stewart Copeland's influence in the way that I played and varied the hi-hat part in the first twelve bars. Like Gadd and Bonham, Copeland is a strong stylistic influence of mine. As artists, they are beautiful reference points.

The filtered drums at bar 93 are actually the drums from the demo, eq'd and filtered into oblivion. It is a nice way to keep the momentum going, while at the same time producing a sonic breakdown. We used a similar idea on the song "Arriving Somewhere But Not Here."

Start of Something Beautiful

♩=160

Steven Wilson, Gavin Harrison

Start of Something Beautiful

Verse

Start of Something Beautiful

Pre-Chorus

Chorus

Verse

Start of Something Beautiful

Guitar Solo

Pre-Chorus

Chorus

Start of Something Beautiful

Filtered Drums

Solo 2

Start of Something Beautiful

Instrumental Bridge

Start of Something Beautiful

Outro

Chorus

I was always very observant as a child, and would often question the things that I heard. Why did this drummer switch to playing the ride at this point? Or why does he play the snare in half-time during the bridge? I wanted to understand the musical reason behind the things that I liked the sound of. I wanted to know why they worked and why other things didn't work (in my opinion).

Between the ages of 13 and 17 I saw a lot of drum clinics (certainly more than 100). My local music shop used to put on a drum clinic every Wednesday. I used to walk to the

shop after school, eat some chips on the way, and watch the clinic. Quite often it was the same guy, Geoff Cox. He was a professional drummer that also worked part time in the shop and was doing it just out of kindness in order to help educate young drummers. Every two or three weeks he would have a guest drummer. I, of course, had nothing else to do on a Wednesday evening so I looked forward to learning something from the clinics. Often, I would get invited on stage to play and demonstrate things. He would use me as his crash test dummy.

I observed and remembered little things that some of the other drummers played that I really liked. I would go home and work on them. I also made a mental note of the things that I didn't like, and thought, "I must remember never to do that."

I suppose all of these observations start to build into a musical personality. The tricks and licks that I've stolen and changed over the years have become my "style." It is just a huge list of influences that are mixed in with my own ideas.

Mother and Child Divided

This is another tune that started off with a drum rhythm. Actually, it is an idea I had while writing my first book, *Rhythmic Illusions* (Ex.124 on page 66, to be precise).

It's basically a pattern of ten notes cut up in the most "spiky" way I could think of. If the pattern repeats three times and two sixteenth notes are added to the end, it all adds up to two bars of 4/4 in sixteenth-note subdivisions. The song is more of an atmospheric piece that is based over heavy guitars and drums playing that odd rhythm, with some keyboard melodies floating over the top.

Steve was at my house one day and I played him this pattern. He really liked it. We wrote a guitar part which followed the drums exactly, and this makes up the basis of the song. When it came time for me to record the drums, I felt that the original drum pattern (taken from my book) was a bit too funky, since the hi-hat part was very syncopated. Now that the song had taken on a much heavier "metal" angle, the hi-hat part needed to be straightened out. I thought a straight eighth-note hi-hat pattern that accented quarter notes would balance the 10+10+10+2 rhythms going on underneath it.

Sometimes (as an extra embellishment), in the extra two sixteenths at the end of the two bar pattern, I'll slip in a double-bass drum triplet.

Although the whole thing is in 4/4, it doesn't really sound like it. Sometimes it's fun to make 4/4 sound like it's in an odd time signature. Similarly, making odd times sound even is something I have utilized a lot. There is a chorus part at bar 25 where I introduce a straighter-sounding 2 & 4 backbeat to provide some contrast.

In the second verse (bar 33), I programmed a metallic percussion sound that basically plays where my ghost notes used to be in the original pattern from the book. It fits into all of the holes between the bass drum and snare drum accents.

Of course, the last four bars are just everyone playing that 10+10+10+2 pattern. I doubled it with a tom sound from Richard's Prophet synth. We've used that "multi-tom" patch on a few things—most recently the tom section in "Octane Twisted." It's a sound that Richard used back in his Japan days, and it always sits really well with real drums.

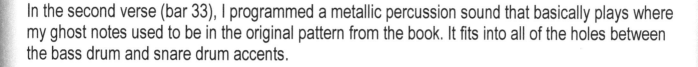

Mother and Child Divided

Steven Wilson, Gavin Harrison

♩=120

Chorus

Verse

Mother and Child Divided

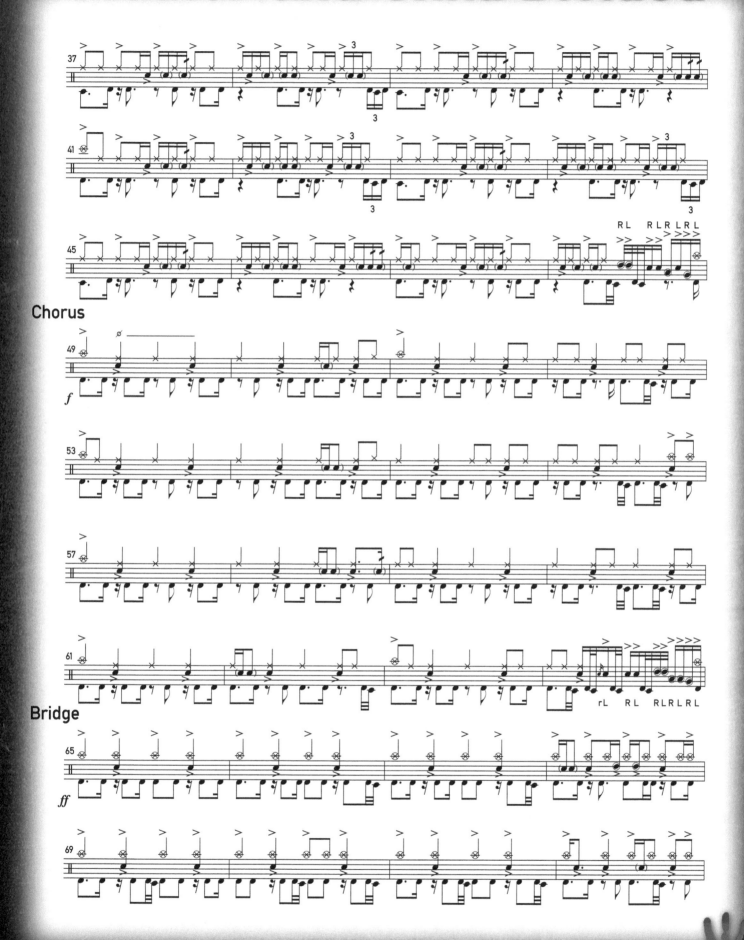

Chorus

Bridge

Mother and Child Divided

Bridge 2

Chorus

Bridge

Mother and Child Divided

Outro

Chapter 4

Fear of a Blank Planet

Fear Of A Blank Planet

After the writing of *Fear Of A Blank Planet*, we thought it would be beneficial to go out and play the songs live in front of an audience. This way we could get some real-time feedback from the crowd before we recorded the material. We did a short, twenty-date tour (starting September 2006), and played six of the new songs: "Fear Of A Blank Planet," "My Ashes," "Anesthetize," "Sentimental," "Cheating the Polygraph" (which we later replaced with "Way Out Of Here"), and "Sleep Together." We performed all six new songs as the first set of the show. After a short break, we would come back and play a selection of our older songs.

Usually, we would record a complete album and then go on tour. After performing the new material for a few weeks, we would start to feel that we were playing the songs much better than the recorded versions. Short tours such as these gave us the chance to smooth out a lot of the transitions in the songs, and find better fills, solos, and dynamics for many of the sections. Our songs still evolved and mutated on the following tours, but the pre-touring gave us a good head start on the process.

The drumset for *Fear Of A Blank Planet* was the same set that I used for the *Deadwing* album. Thanks to the pleasing results of the *Deadwing* sessions, I recorded the drums at home again—only this time I knew what I wanted to play so it was very quick and easy.

Anesthetize

"A nesthetize" is a song in three parts. The section that is transcribed here is the last 33 bars of the first part. This section then segues into "The Pills I'm Taking," which is the second part. It's probably one of the songs we've played live the most (247 times according to a setlist website).

This is a very high energy song to play; I certainly have to save up some strength to really hit it at full force every night. Steve presented us with the song basically written, and there are some tricky sections to navigate. For instance, the guitar riffs that start at bar 34 are quite asymmetrical. I played over them many times at home trying to find a way that I could catch some of the accents and make rhythmical sense of the phrase. I wanted to fit in some double-bass-drum embellishments to the riffs without sounding too distracting.

Originally, the riff didn't return after the first chorus, but I liked it so much I suggested that it could come back at bar 88—but played only twice instead of four times like the start. Then we could drop out and leave Steve singing the beginning of the next verse on his own. We felt that it would be a great contrast. Once the verse groove gets going, it's a real "rolling freight train" kind of effect with the guitars, bass, and sequencer playing syncopated sixteenth-note patterns. In the second verse, I added open hi-hat notes on all four quarter notes, but the hi-hat only opens for an eighth note in duration. It kind of sounds like an industrial pump, pushing the rhythm along.

The part I spent longest on was the instrumental section at bar 156. There was a completely blank canvas there for me to steer through those guitar riffs. It left a lot of decisions to be made from my point of view. I felt that it was best to play the first bar-and-a-half pretty straight, and then peel away to start catching some of the accents towards the end of the riff. I must have tried a hundred different ideas until I settled on the final one. That's the joy of having your own studio: being able to spend as much time as you want on any idea.

The bridge is a special moment. It is one that I was very pleased to find an easy solution to. Steve had always imagined this part as being flat-out wild. I had already thought of making a 4-over-3 polyrhythm with the snare and bass drums (by playing two hits on the bass drum with my right foot in between dotted eighth notes on the snare drum). When I added the extra subdivisions with my left foot, it really sounded crazy (at least for me it did). Some folks thought I was playing continuous thirty second notes on the bass drums, but as you can see, it's just short bursts of four equal notes. This meant that I could play them accurately and for a sustained amount of time. It is something that I wouldn't have been able to do if I had played continuous thirty second notes through that section (I'm really not much of a double-bass-drum player).

Anesthetize

Steven Wilson

65

Anesthetize

Anesthetize

Chorus

Verse

Anesthetize

Chorus

Bridge

Anesthetize

Keyboard Solo

Instrumental

Anesthetize

Way Out of Here

Originally, this song came out of a band writing session many months before. As I stated earlier, the six songs that we played live before recording were easy to capture in the studio, because we'd already ironed out most of the wrinkles. However, we hadn't rehearsed and played "Way Out Of Here," so it was a big challenge to make it sound as polished as the other songs. I spent a lot of time on this one, and there were a lot of options available to play with.

The song is basically in 6/8, but I wanted the first verse to feel more like 3/4, so the chorus would have a contrasting feel to it. These meters (3/4 and 6/8) are basically the same thing; it just depends how you feel it. When you accent quarter notes and omit the snare drum accent on the fourth eighth note, it feels more like 3/4. When you accent every three eighth notes and place a snare drum accent on the fourth, it feels more like 6/8.

The second bridge, at measure 129, is another variation on the same idea. This time, the right hand plays the 3/4 feel on the hi-hat, while the left hand and feet are in the 6/8 feel.

The outro section is a bit of an octopus job, with the right hand moving quickly from the ride cymbal to the toms, while the left hand is doing a similar thing between the snare drum and toms. Both hands are following a definite 6/8 feel, while the feet have gone back to the 3/4 pattern. When we started playing this song live, we built the end section up into more of a frenzy. It was just one of those things that evolved over many nights of performing. It's quite an epic piece, with lots of changes in direction and dynamics.

Way Out of Here

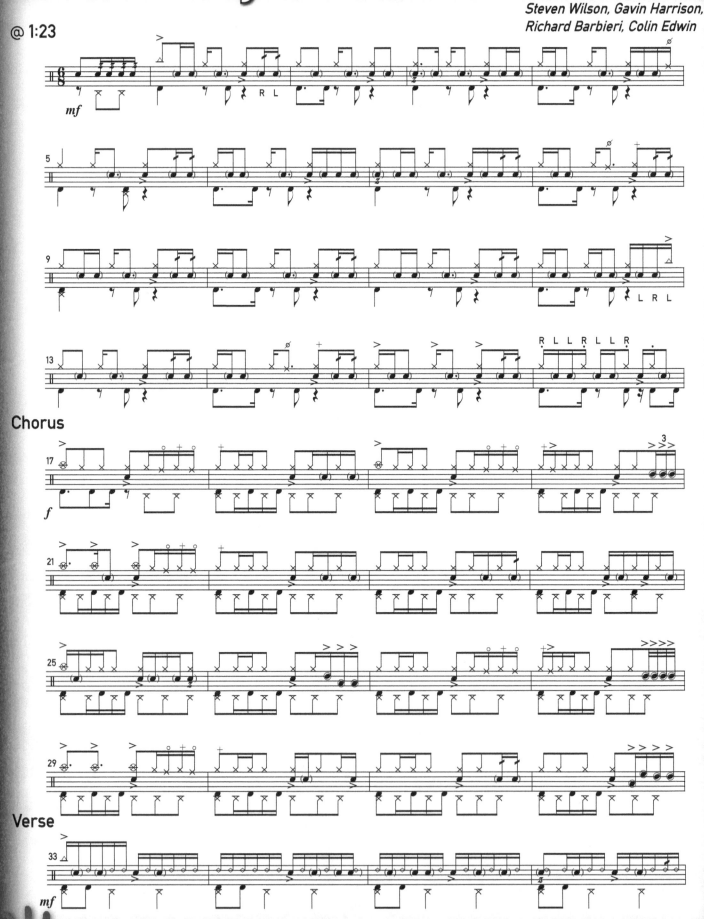

Way Out of Here

Chorus

Way Out of Here

Guitar Solo

Bridge

Way Out of Here

Bridge 2

Drum Solo

Chorus

Way Out of Here

Outro

Way Out of Here

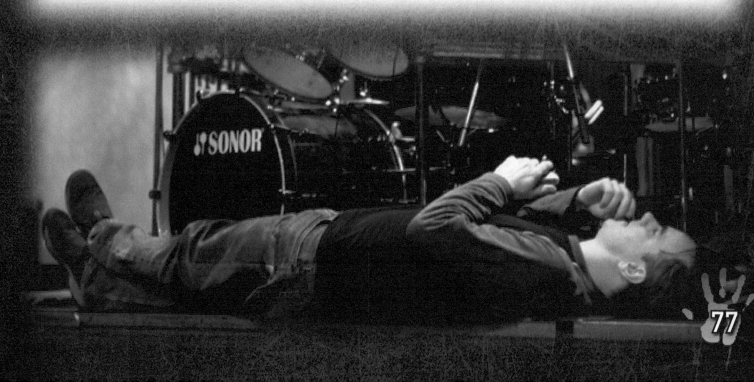

Chapter 5

Nil Recurring

Nil Recurring

I have owned guitars and basses for many years, but I never really got around to learning to play them with any real conviction. I'll occasionally pick one of them up and start tapping and banging around on it—usually from a percussive starting point, rather than anything particularly melodic or harmonic. One such day, I tapped out what you hear at the intro of this tune. I then counter-balanced it with a second guitar line (at 0:17). It was a good lesson in always making sure that you tune up the guitar before you start recording. You never know if your demo guitar line might end up on the finished record (as in this case). It was a demo that I intended to play to the other PT guys as a starting point for a writing session. Sometimes these things are fruitful and other times not. There are plenty of PT demos sitting in the virtual trash can that we just couldn't quite get off the ground and develop into something that we all liked. Such is the nature of composition.

After the tapping guitar intro got recorded, I tried some drum ideas out and settled on a kind of polyrhythmic blend between 6/8 and 3/4 (depending on how you hear it). You'll see it written here as 6/8, but the hi-hat is playing more of a 3/4 rhythm (three equal open hi-hat notes across the 6/8 bar). Colin and Steve came up with a great heavy riff that became an anchor for the tune. There is plenty of room for me to go nuts on this song.

Doing my "Popeye arms" impersonation.

In contrast to the heavy section, there's a beautiful haunting atmospheric solo section that comes in at bar 57. It really gives Richard some space to explore with his synth sounds along with Robert Fripp's soundscapes. In fact, Robert returns later in the song to rip it up with a wailing guitar solo. He said that the solo starting at measure 141 took a few years off of his life!

I can hear my lovely old Avedis Zildjian 1940s 20" ride cymbal in there. It makes me regret the breaking of it even more.

We played this song a few times live, and had a really nice film to accompany it, but somehow it didn't really knock us out that much when we performed it. I still enjoy hearing the energy of the recorded version.

Nil Recurring

♪=170

Steven Wilson, Gavin Harrison,
Richard Barbieri, Colin Edwin

Intro

Heavy Riff

Nil Recurring

Heavy Riff 2

Solo Section

Nil Recurring

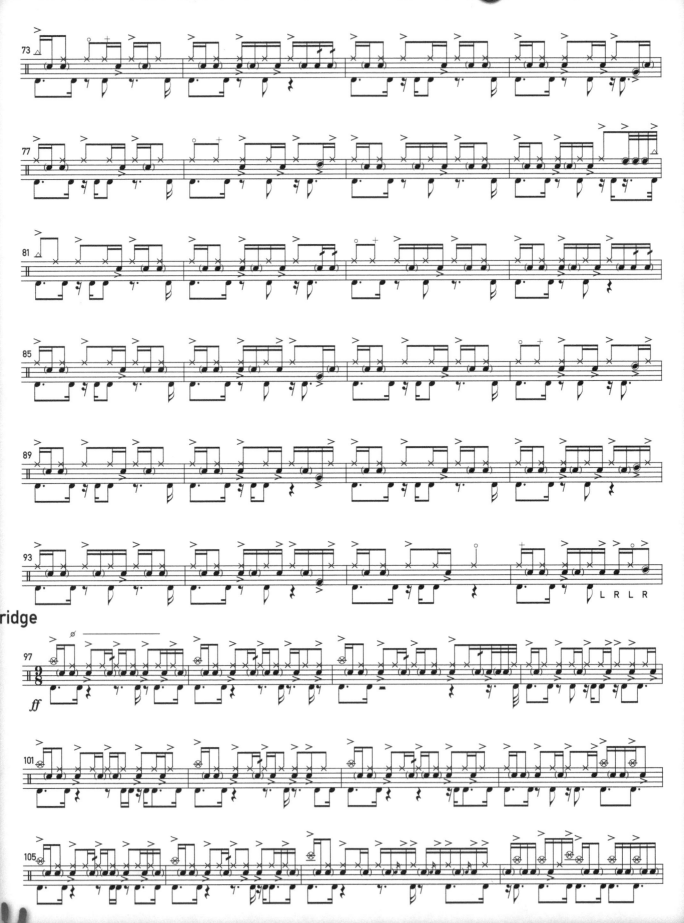

Bridge

Nil Recurring

Middle Section

Nil Recurring

Outro

Outro Solo

Cheating The Polygraph

This is a song that was originally intended for the *Fear Of A Blank Planet* album. We played it live (along with the other five songs) before recording it. It has a very unusual verse rhythm that some folks thought was some kind of a shuffle. The truth is this rhythm is in a fast 7/8. The bass drum is on the first part of a 7/16 group, and the snare drum backbeat is on the start of the second 7/16 group. This evenly-spaced downbeat and backbeat give a strange familiarity to the rhythm. Steve sings it like it's in a very loose, floating 6/8—as if he's just hearing the equidistant downbeat and backbeat. If you don't really hear all the subdivisions I might forgive you for thinking it was a half-time shuffle feel. This rhythmic

"Believe me, it's not a shuffle."

misdirection was (of course) deliberate, and something we wanted to surprise people with. Sometimes it's fun to manipulate people's perception of where and how they hear the beat.

The chorus goes into a more energetic-feeling 5/8. It feels more hectic because of the regularity and pace of the snare accents. This is in stark contrast to the verse where the backbeats are much more spread out. It has a more laid-back, relaxed feel to it.

I have often used this method to design verse and chorus patterns (as with "Start of Something Beautiful"). I want to have that mellow feel in the verse with a much more exciting-sounding chorus. Sometimes it's just a question of how close the snare accents are to each other. In this case, there's also a compression of time signatures: the verse is in 7/8 and the chorus is in 5/8.

This song was always challenging to play live from a concentration and stamina point of view. It was one of those songs where I knew I was going to need to take a good deep breath before we set off. After playing it on the short tour to preview the new songs, we decided to drop it from the main album and put "Way Out of Here" on there instead.

There is a quarter-note override on the open hi-hat at bar 201, to give the 5/8 a different slant. The end is based on a 5/8 sixteenth-note-triplet pattern that I use on another tune (which I used to play on drum clinics) called "Slippin' Away Part 2." On that tune, the 5/8 in sixteenth-note triplets lasted for four bars of 4/4. On "Cheating The Polygraph," it was just straight patterns of 5/8 without superimposing them over another time signature. Every time we've gone out and played a really hard song live, the first night is full of paranoia that we're never going to get through it. After we've done it a few times, we can't believe why we were so nervous about it.

It was recorded at my home studio late 2006 on the Sonor earth finish drumset.

Cheating The Polygraph

♩=112

Steven Wilson, Gavin Harrison

Verse

Verse

Cheating The Polygraph

Chorus

Cheating The Polygraph

Solo Section

Verse

Chorus

Cheating The Polygraph

Instrumental

Cheating The Polygraph

Guitar Solo

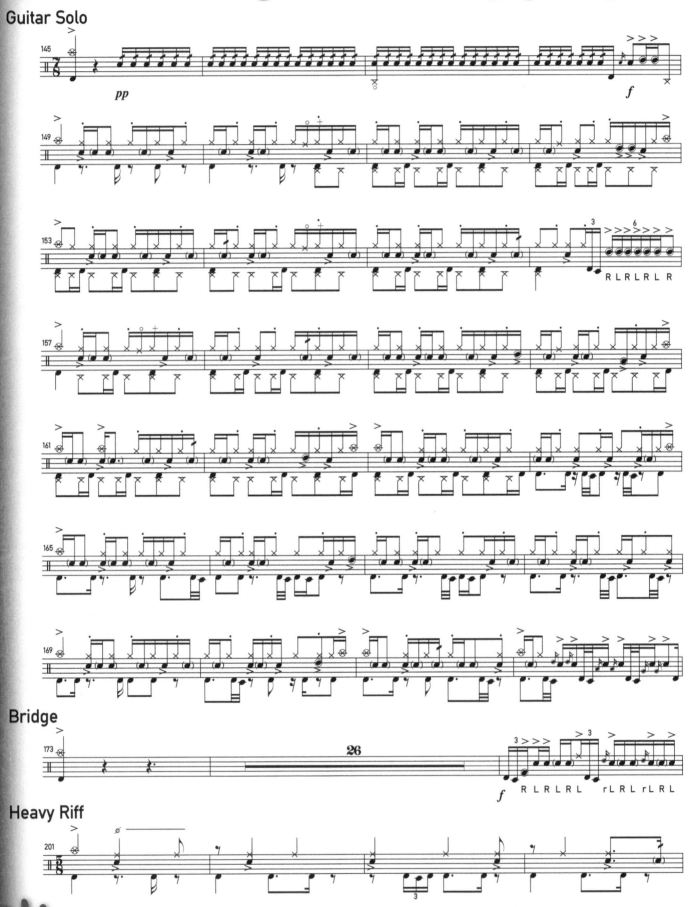

Bridge

Heavy Riff

Cheating The Polygraph

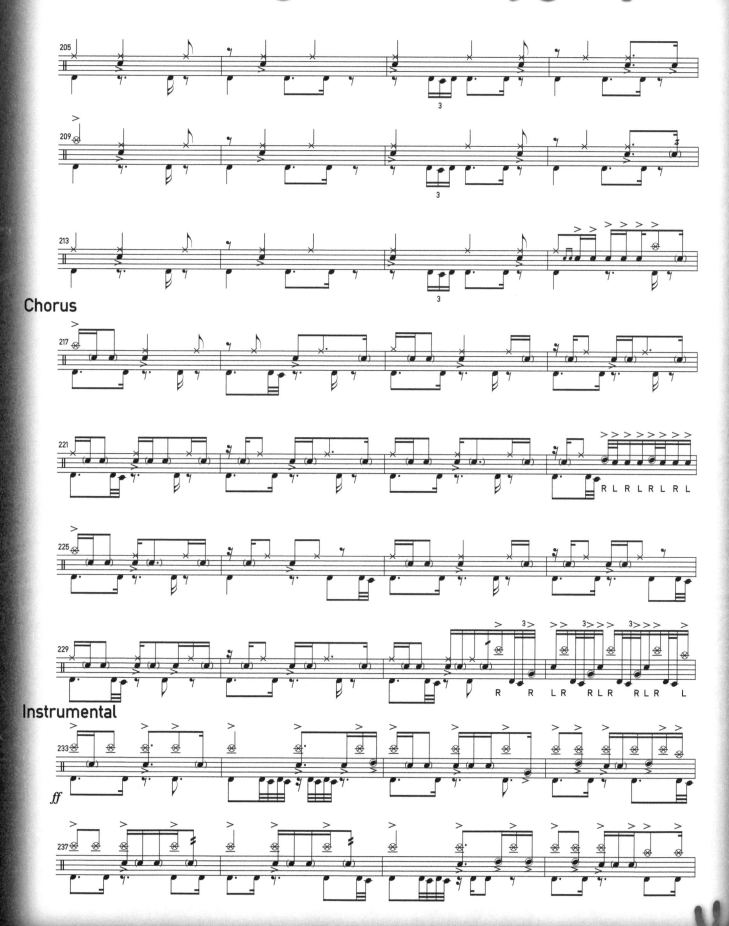

Chorus

Instrumental

Cheating The Polygraph

Outro

"I think I can see the dressing room from here."

What Happens Now?

During a band writing session for the *Nil Recurring* EP, I looked in my percussion cupboard and pulled out a Remo Sound Shape with a long spring attached. I had seen it in a drum shop a few years before. Whenever I see some percussive contraption that captures my imagination, I buy it. You never know when it might inspire something. It sounds like a tiny hand drum with a funky built-in reverb (because of the spring). I picked up a pencil and started tapping out a rhythm on it.

Richard really liked it, so I recorded eight bars into my computer, and assigned it to the left speaker. Then I recorded a slightly different eight bars, assigned it to the right speaker, and made a loop out of it. Richard played some chords along to it and we all started to like where it was going. I jumped on the drums, and Colin and I started to play along. That's basically the section at bar 41. It's a nice, straight, and easy-going groove.

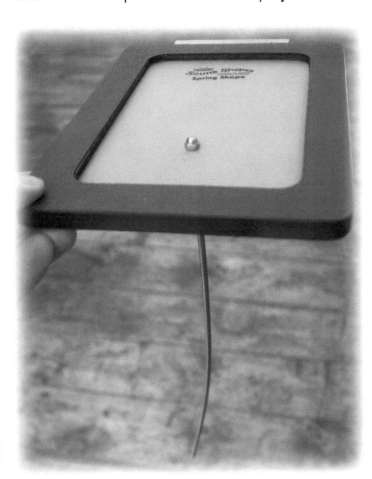

Steve suggested a bridge section that moved away from the chord cycle that we had been playing on, and that brought us to the outro section. We thought that it should change direction dramatically here, so I raised my hand and said that I had a strange idea. I've always been rhythmically curious, and a few days earlier I had an idea about making a 3-D rhythm.

My plan was to use the 5/8 guitar loop from "Anesthetize" to start off with—and slightly mislead the listener (why shouldn't we have recurring themes?). Then I would play a polyrhythm in 7/8, but with an override of 3/16 on the ride cymbal. I wanted Colin to just listen to my bass drum and snare pattern, and play a bass line in 7/8. After a certain amount of time, Richard would follow the 3/16 on the ride cymbal and play as if it were a different tempo (disregarding the bass line and kick and snare parts). Meanwhile, Steve would play a picked guitar part that was based in 6/16 that would (at a pre-determined point) join Richard with the 3/16 melody. As a final payoff, we would abandon the 7/8 feel and all join the 3/16 rhythm. It would then modulate into a 6/8 triplet blues feel in a related tempo (bar 134). Time for a big guitar solo, perhaps? Actually, on the record it's an electric violin solo.

What Happens Now?

The hardest part for me was not the polyrhythm, but the fact that Colin's 7/8 part was following a four-bar chord cycle. My polyrhythm resolved itself every three bars of 7/8, so there was a bit of a headache in trying to hit a crash after every fourth 7/8 bar; it would sometimes land in an awkward place in relation to my polyrhythm. I sat down with pencil and paper and worked out where all the predetermined changes should happen from a mathematical/rhythmical point of view. I then explained to everyone how many times they should repeat their part before moving on to the next section.

Obviously, I wanted the big transition at bar 134 to be the point where all the cycles resolved, so I had to work backwards from that. Mad idea? Quite possibly. Hardest thing we ever tried to do live? Absolutely!

I was very excited about it because I hadn't heard a band attempt anything quite like this before, and it was a new thing for PT. It definitely gave us some worrying moments in rehearsals and soundchecks, where it would occasionally fall apart. There's a look of great relief on some of our faces when we pulled it off without a hitch on the *Anesthetize* DVD.

♩=112 What Happens Now?

Steven Wilson, Gavin Harrison,
Richard Barbieri, Colin Edwin

@ 1:44

Verse

Chorus

What Happens Now?

Instrumental

+ Guitar

What Happens Now?

Bridge

Outro

What Happens Now?

What Happens Now?

Chapter 6

The Incident

The Incident

As time rolls by working in my studio, I often crave the chance to work in other studios—especially if they're really good ones. One of my all time favorites is right here in London: AIR Studios, situated in Hampstead. I've worked there before and was *very* impressed. The 2002 orchestra session for *In Absentia* was recorded in the big hall there. I had previously done some soundtrack work in studio one there as well. That was the room I really wanted for the drum sound.

We lined up five days at AIR. I would start work at about 10:30 in the morning, and then Steve would come in around 7:00 at night (just as I'd pretty much burnt myself out for the day). In this way, he could take advantage of their beautiful grand piano and the great engineer Steve Orchard. The acoustic guitars got recorded there as well.

I had rehearsed extensively at home, because I knew I didn't have the luxury of open-ended time at AIR. I pressed on and got the whole thing finished quite quickly.

It felt good to go to work at AIR studios because it's such an amazing place, but it also really drove me to get this album finished quickly. At home I would probably have taken a couple of weeks to record the same songs. It was a different way of recording for us, and that's probably a good thing. It feels like you're moving on and doing something new.

The drumset was my black-and-white tribal finish Sonor SQ2: 22x17 bass drum, 8x7, 10x8, and 12x9 mounted toms. The floor toms were 15x13 and 16x14.

Drawing The Line

This was a fun song to play, and it gave me chance to design a drum part that I was happy with. It was surprisingly challenging to play, mainly in making all those ghost notes on the snare drum feel right. I think I played them hand-to-hand on the recording, but during the tour I found that I could play them a bit more smoothly using only the right hand. I wanted the drum part to have a melody that counter-balanced the vocals.

The drum part in the verse reminds me of a groove that I played on "La Cura," a terrific song by Franco Battiato. I was happy with the way that song turned out, and probably in my subconscious I was channeling it for this PT song. I like the fact that there's no hi-hat or cymbals in the verse. It makes the chorus explode a little more when the cymbals finally come crashing in.

This photo is from an open-air show that was infested with mosquitoes—hence the long-sleeved shirt. They still bit me, though!

Drawing The Line

♩=78

Steven Wilson

(Half-Time Feel)

Verse

Chorus (Double-Time Feel)

Drawing The Line

Instrumental

Verse   (Half-Time Feel)

mf   Mic Hit

Chorus   (Double-Time Feel)

Drawing The Line

The Incident

This simple song is about a road accident. The police are usually vague about what has happened at these things, and put up road signs simply saying "incident." Steve saw a scene like this while in a traffic jam on a motorway, and it inspired the lyrics for the song.

The first couple of minutes have a small-sounding programmed drum loop. When the real drums come in at 2:22, the contrast is large and powerful.

I experimented with some drum parts that might work, and the thing I liked the most was a little unusual. I followed the heavy guitar riff with two snare hits halfway through the bar. I wanted to slightly vary where the first snare hit in the bar would come in, as you will see in the transcription. The chorus is fairly straightforward, and the bass drum pattern seems to drive it in a flowing way.

The Incident

The Incident

Instrumental

Chorus

Octane Twisted

This song (along with "Circle of Manias" and "Remember Me Lover") came out of a band writing session in December of 2008.

In the first sixteen bars, the right hand plays the quarter notes on the ride cymbal, but it also comes back to the snare drum and plays some of the in-between ghost notes.

The riff is basically 5+5+3+3 (=16) x 2 and then 7+9 (also =16). The section sounds very much like an odd time signature, but in fact it all adds up to 4/4. It's always fun to make 4/4 feel "odd" and, likewise, make "odd" time signatures feel "even."

Giving the hi-hat the death stare.

Octane Twisted

♩=95

Steven Wilson, Gavin Harrison,
Richard Barbieri, Colin Edwin

@ 1:00

Riff

Instrumental

Octane Twisted

Riff

Instrumental 2

Outro

Octane Twisted

Circle of Manias

This piece was another one that came from the band writing session in late 2008. It makes a nice contrast to have these heavy interludes on *The Incident*. The entire album was written as one long, continuous piece in fourteen parts. The dynamic differences between quite etherial pieces such as "The Yellow Windows" and heavier songs like "Circle Of Manias" are quite extreme. It's something that we have always liked.

The first half of the piece is a riff in 9/8. I try to find some different ways to drive the groove. By the time it gets to bar nine, there is an override on the open hi-hat to give the listener the feeling of a slower quarter-note feel.

Circle of Manias

♩=95

Heavy Riff

Steven Wilson, Gavin Harrison,
Richard Barbieri, Colin Edwin

Riff 2

Breakdown

Heavy Riff

Circle of Manias

Bonnie The Cat

This is another song that started with the drum pattern. I was improvising on my drums at home (as I do virtually every day I'm there), and I stumbled across parts of a pattern that I liked. As is so often the case, the moment of creation is the moment when I recognize that something new is happening, rather than all the familiar waffle that I've played many times before. I'm very happy if I can come up with something that I don't think I've played before—and can't recall anyone else playing either. Creating an original rhythm in 4/4 is quite a challenge these days, when you think of how many songs exist in 4/4. Nobody is more familiar (and bored) with my drumming than I am, so when I start to notice something new, I latch onto it quickly. In fact, I grabbed my little video camera and pressed record so I could at least get some of it down before it disappeared into the ether or I'd forget some detail about it (it's all about the details folks!). I enjoy feeling like I'm walking on new ground, even if it turns out to be just the same old ground but with new shoes on.

I transcribed the pattern from the improvisation so I could see exactly where all the beats were landing. The two figures that had caught my ear were the open hi-hats on beats 2 and 3 (of the first bar) and the tom-to-snare accents at the end of bar two. I just needed to fill in the holes and make some sense of it. I probably played around with it for about an hour until I settled on the verse pattern that you see in the transcription.

I liked that there was quite often no bass drum on the "one." It needed to have the right amount of snare drum backbeats in there to have a balance. If there are too many of them close together, then the ship becomes unbalanced and starts lilting to one side. If the snare accents are regular 2 & 4, it gives the groove a completely different kind of momentum. I prefer to save the 2 & 4 backbeat for later in the song when things might need to be a bit

straighter. If the snare drum backbeats were on beat 3, it would give the song a lumbering half-time feel. Knowing where to place snare drum accents in a bar is quite an art—and one that I learned a lot from drummer Steve Jansen. In some places within the bar, the snare accent will help propel you along. In other places it will feel like it's holding things back. Some will imply a different feel.

The "rhythmic design" of a song is very much in partnership with the bass player. I was always influenced by the "rhythmic designs" of Steve Jansen and (bassist) Mick Karn. They quite often didn't play together, but in between each other. I wanted to have a kind of jigsaw rhythm part on this song. I grabbed my bass guitar and jammed along with the drums, looking for rhythmic holes I could get in between. During the band writing session in December 2008, I played my demo for the other PT guys. They responded positively. We worked on the idea for about a day and a half before we whittled it into some kind of shape that Steve could think about putting vocals over.

Bonnie The Cat

♩=110

Steven Wilson, Gavin Harrison,
Richard Barbieri, Colin Edwin

Bonnie The Cat

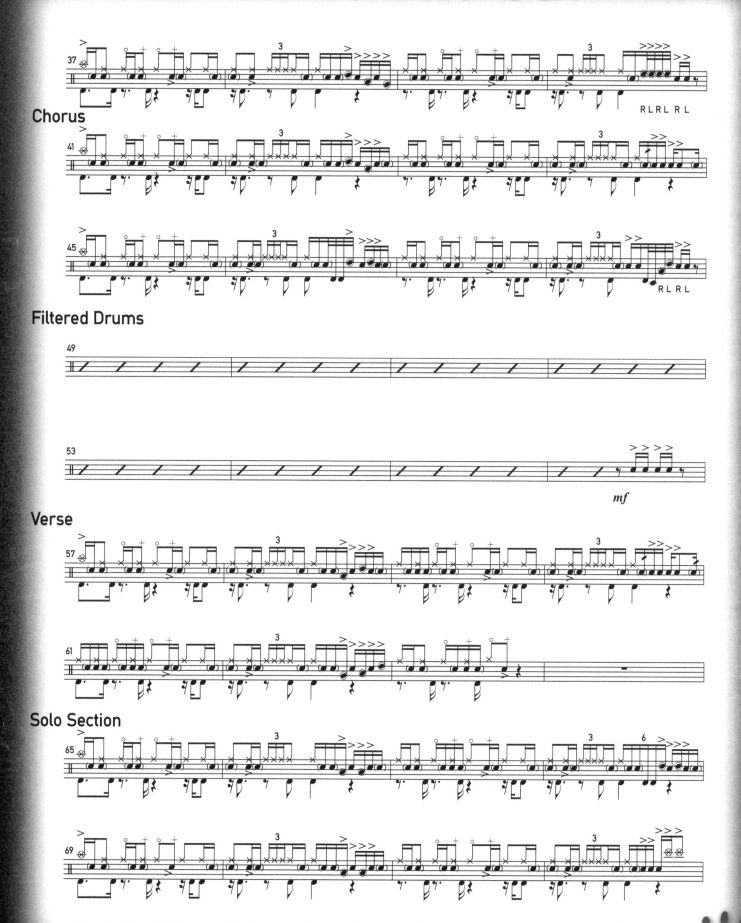

Chorus

Filtered Drums

Verse

Solo Section

Bonnie The Cat

Bonnie The Cat

Outro 2

Remember Me Lover

The rumbling hand-drum sound before the drum kit enters is my original Mark 1 Korg WaveDrum, which came out of retirement for this song. I brought it with me on the writing session and found inspiration to play it in the verses. It lends a strange lo-fi percussive element to the rhythm.

This song has a simple, straightforward verse, bridge, and chorus that moves between 4/4 and 3/4 time. I decided to bring back the pumping open hi-hat feel for the heavy riff sections. It's all pretty laid-back until we get to bar 158, where everything doubles in feel and weight. There is a very powerful ending to this song. It was originally intended to be the end of the record, but we enjoy ending with a ballad, so we decided that "I Drive The Hearse" would finish off the *Incident* album.

♩=133 Remember Me Lover

Steven Wilson

@ 1:50

Chorus

Bridge

Remember Me Lover

Heavy Riff

Remember Me Lover

Chorus

Bridge

Remember Me Lover

Heavy Riff

Outro

Remember Me Lover

Acknowledgments

Gavin would like to thank:

Karl Heinz Menzel, Stefan Althoff, Thomas Barth, David Schulz, and Michael Stumm at Sonor drums.
Tina Clarke, Bob Wiczling, and Sarah Hagen at Zildjian cymbals.
Joe Testa and Ben Davies at Vic Firth sticks.
Adam Murphy at Remo.
Dave Eyre at Hardcase.
Aaron Vishria for Tama Speed Cobra pedals.
Dil Davies and Paul Barretta for the Porter&Davies BC2.
Ken Fredenberg and Brent Barnett at Gibraltar hardware.
Hannah LB Schoenholtz.

Terry would like to thank:

Everyone who purchased this book.
All at Hudson Music and Hal Leonard.
Bernhard Castiglioni at drummerworld.com.
All at *Modern Drummer* magazine.
Gavin for all of the help.
Porcupine Tree for all of the great music.
All of my students for the constant inspiration.
Erin Branam for her incredible support and patience.

Photo Credits:

Diana Nitschke: pages 6, 13, 18, 26, 37, 42, 45, 47, 56, 61, 64, 79, 85, 92, 93, 102, 107, 110, 113, 116, 117
Claudia Hahn: pages 17, 71, 85, 103, 109, 114, 122
Lasse Hoile: front cover, pages 9, 22, 28, 29, 57, 77, 95, 102
Bob Wiczling: pages 14, 48, 55, 100
Joe Del Tufo: page 63
Helmo Hudson: page 7